Take a Stand!®

Ancient Civilizations

Reading, Discussing, and Writing

by John De Gree

Take a Stand Publications
San Clemente, California

DEDICATION

Dedicated to students willing to take a stand

Table of Contents

Part One: Social Studies Curriculum

Part Two: Social Studies Literacy Curriculum

Part One: Social Studies Curriculum

Chapter I: One-Paragraph Response Essays

1. Early Human Civilizations

In the Old Stone Age (also called the Paleolithic Age), humans lived in hunter-gatherer societies. These early people followed herds of animals making sure to stay close to the main food source. Typically, men hunted animals while women gathered wild berries, nuts, and grains. These peoples are known as nomads because they did not have a permanent home, but rather they continuously wandered, searching for food and water.

In a time known as the New Stone Age (Neolithic Age), humans began to live in permanent homes, ending their nomadic lives. Humans were able to domesticate their own animals, plant crops, and provide clothing and shelter without following wild animals. Once in permanent homes with enough food to live on, humans had more time to develop better tools and to think about science, nature, religion, government, and philosophy. The change from a hunter-gatherer society to an agricultural society was a drastic one.

In a one-paragraph essay, answer the question, "What allowed humans to change from being nomads to having permanent homes?" Choose two causes that you consider most important.

This essay has six assignments:

Assignment	Due Date		Due Date
1. Prewriting Activities	_____	4. Works Cited	_____
2. Thesis Statement	_____	5. Rough Draft	_____
3. Outline	_____	6. Final	_____

Prewriting Activities for Assignment #1

A. The Environment

1. What was the Ice Age?_____
_____

2. When was the Ice Age?_____
_____

3. After the Ice Age ended, what was different on Earth?_____
_____

4. How did man change his life after the Ice Age ended?_____
_____

5. Why do historians say the Ice Age happened in a prehistoric period?_____
_____

B. Human Discoveries and Inventions

1. Name one discovery during the New Stone Age that helped people become farmers.___
_____

2. Name one discovery that allowed man to have light when it was dark outside, kept man warm, and cooked food._____
_____

3. What discovery of man cut stones to be used as tools?_____
_____

4. What helped man kill animals?_____
_____

5. Which invention helped early man store food?_____
_____

C. Rate the Importance

Rate the importance of the inventions and discoveries, and explain your rating.	
1.	1.
2.	2.
3.	3.
4.	4.
5.	5.

C. Class Discussion

When you share ideas with other students, your ideas may be reinforced, rejected, or slightly changed. Listening to your classmates' ideas will help you form your own judgment.

Each student must interview at least three classmates who do not sit next to one another. The answers to the following questions must be written down on a piece of paper.

    1. What is your name?
    2. What do you think were the two most important discoveries or inventions of early man that made it possible for people to stop being nomads and have permanent homes?
    3. Which evidence do you have that supports what you think?

Reflection

After you have written down all your classmates' responses, think about them and ask yourself the following questions. Write down your answers under your classmates' responses.

    1. What do I think of my classmates' answers?
    2. Which two reasons do I think are the main ones that made early man able to leave the nomadic lifestyle and have one home?
    3. Did my answers change after I spoke with my classmates?
    4. If they changed, why did they and how did they?

You should now have a chance to present your ideas in a class discussion. If somebody says something with which you disagree, speak up! In your discussion, you may find out they are actually right and you are wrong. All possible viewpoints should be stated and defended out loud. Test your ideas in class.

2. Mesopotamia, Egypt, and Kush

Many of the world's earliest civilizations were located in Mesopotamia and Egypt. The great rivers of the Nile, the Euphrates, and the Tigris were centers of these societies, which have given mankind great contributions. Spanning from about the year 4000 B.C. to 350 A.D., incredible inventions, discoveries, and new ways of thought emerged from these lands.

In a well-developed one-paragraph essay, answer the question "What are the two most important contributions to the world made by the ancient civilizations of Mesopotamia, Egypt, and Kush?" Explain which civilization is responsible for the contributions you choose, and explain how these contributions are important to us today.

This essay has six assignments:

Assignment	Due Date		Due Date
1. Prewriting Activities	_____	4. Works Cited	_____
2. Thesis Statement	_____	5. Rough Draft	_____
3. Outline	_____	6. Final	_____

Prewriting Activities for Assignment #2
A. Ancient Civilizations of Mesopotamia, Egypt, and Kush

Research the greatest contributions of civilizations of Mesopotamia, Egypt, and Kush. Write fifteen contributions, which civilization was responsible for them, and what this contribution means to world civilizations today. Below are listed the major ancient civilizations of Mesopotamia, Egypt, and Kush.

Sumeria (c. 4000–2300 B.C.)   **Babylonia** (c. 2300–1600 B.C.)
Hittite (c. 1600–1200 B.C.)   **Phoenicia** (c. 1200–146 B.C.)
Hebrew (c. 1200–600 B.C.)   **Assyria** (c. 1100–650 B.C.)
Chaldea (c. 605–539 B.C.)   **Persia** (c. 550–330 B.C.)
Ancient Egypt (c. 3000–343 B.C.)   **Kush** (c. 1070 B.C.–A.D. 350)

CONTRIBUTIONS	
Contributions	**Civilization**
1._____	1._____
2._____	2._____
3._____	3._____
4._____	4._____
5._____	5._____
6._____	6._____
7._____	7._____
8._____	8._____
9._____	9._____
10._____	10._____
11._____	11._____
12._____	12._____
13._____	13._____
14._____	14._____
15._____	15._____

B. Rating the Contributions

Rate the contributions of the various civilizations of Mesopotamia, Egypt, and Kush. Which contribution do you think is the most important? Which is the second most important? Write the origin of the contribution. From which civilization did it come?

Contributions in order of importance	Civilization
1.	1.
2.	2.
3.	3.
4.	4.
5.	5.
6.	6.
7.	7.
8.	8.
9.	9.
10.	10.
11.	11.
12.	12.
13.	13.
14.	14.
15.	15.

Question
What made you decide which were the top three contributions made to world civilizations?_____
_____
_____
_____

C. Class Discussion

When you share ideas with other students, your ideas may be reinforced, rejected, or slightly changed. Listening to your classmates' ideas will help you form your own judgment.

Each student must interview at least three classmates who do not sit next to one another. The answers to the following questions must be written down on a piece of paper.

1. What is your name?
2. What do you think are the two most important contributions to the world from ancient Mesopotamia, ancient Egypt, and Kush?
3. Why do you think this?

Reflection

After you have written down all your classmates' responses, think about them and ask yourself the following questions. Write down your answers under your classmates' responses.

1. What do I think of these classmates' answers?
2. Which are the three best answers?
3. Have I changed the way I think? How?

You should now have a chance to present your ideas in a class discussion. If somebody says something with which you disagree, speak up! In your discussion, you may find out they are actually right and you are wrong. All possible viewpoints should be stated and defended out loud. Test your ideas in class.

3. Ancient Hebrews

In the middle of a large number of civilizations that practiced similar religious beliefs, one group of people emerged which, in many ways, was completely different than its neighbors. The ancient Hebrews, when compared to neighbors such as the Egyptians, the Phoenicians, and the Assyrians, stood out as a distinct group when it came to issues of ethical teachings (what is right and wrong) and central beliefs (religion).

Although the ancient Hebrews were in the minority, many of their beliefs and ideas are reflected in Western civilization today. In many ways, beliefs and ideas of the ancient Hebrews are very similar to beliefs and ideas of modern Americans. In your essay, answer the question, "What are two most important contributions the ancient Hebrews of the Old Testament gave to Western civilization?"

This essay has six assignments:

Assignment	Due Date		Due Date
1. Prewriting Activities	_____	4. Works Cited	_____
2. Thesis Statement	_____	5. Rough Draft	_____
3. Outline	_____	6. Final	_____

Prewriting Activities for Essay #3
A. What is Western Civilization?

When historians use the term "Western civilization," they are normally talking about societies that share certain ideas and practices together. Many of these ideas and practices came from ancient peoples like the Hebrews, the Greeks, and the Romans. Some of these ideas are a belief in one God (historians call this monotheism), democracy, a society governed by laws, political equality, justice, freedom, and respect for written language.

In this prewriting activity, your goal is to find the continents of the world that are typically associated with being part of Western civilization. By using your textbook, your teacher, your classmates' knowledge, and asking any adult you think may know the answer, complete the following activities. The Hebrews were the first to practice monotheism. The Greeks were the first to practice democracy.

Belief in One God
List the continents where most of the people believe there is one God.

Democracy
List the continents where citizens vote for their leaders.

Look on a map. The continents that you have listed in both categories are typically known as Western civilization.

B. Ancient Hebrew Beliefs

Ancient Hebrew beliefs and ideas have had a profound effect on Western civilization. In this activity, read these written laws from the Hebrews, known as the Ten Commandments. Rewrite them, using your own words, and choose two you think are the most important.

The Ten Commandments

1. I, the Lord, am your God. You shall not have other gods besides me.
2. You shall not take the name of the Lord, your God, in vain.
3. Remember to keep holy the Sabbath day.
4. Honor your father and your mother.
5. You shall not kill.
6. You shall not commit adultery.
7. You shall not steal.
8. You shall not bear false witness against your neighbor.
9. You shall not covet your neighbor's wife.
10. You shall not covet anything that belongs to your neighbor.

Write these in your own words.
1.
2.
3.
4.
5.
6.
7.
8.
9.
10.

QUESTION: Which two do you think are the most important? Why?_____
_____
_____

C. Contributions of Ancient Hebrews

Using your textbook, write down five contributions the ancient Hebrews have made to Western civilization.

Contributions
1.
2.
3.
4.
5.

Prioritize
List these five in order of importance.
1.
2.
3.
4.
5.

Question: Why did you list the top two as being most important? _____

_____

_____

D. Class Discussion

When you share ideas with other students, your ideas may be reinforced, rejected, or slightly changed. Listening to your classmates' ideas will help you form your own judgment.

Each student must interview at least three classmates who do not sit next to one another. The answers to the following questions must be written down on a piece of paper.

    1. What is your name?
    2. What are two of the most important contributions the ancient Hebrews of the Old Testament have made to Western civilization?
    3. Why do you think this?

Reflection

After you have written down all your classmates' responses, think about them and ask yourself the following questions. Write down your answers under your classmates' responses.

    1. What do I think of my classmates' answers?
    2. Which are the best answers to question #2 above?
    3. Have I changed the way I think?
    4. How have I changed the way I think?

You should now have a chance to present your ideas in a classroom discussion. If somebody says something with which you disagree, speak up! In your discussion, you may find out they are actually right, and you are wrong. All possible viewpoints should be said and defended out loud. Test your ideas in class.

4. Judaism

The history of Judaism in the Old Testament is rich in historical and heroic figures. Abraham, Moses, Naomi, Ruth, David, and Yochann ben Zaccai have done much to build and preserve the Jewish faith. Considering that this religion has lasted approximately 4000 years and has affected multiple nations of various continents, these people could possibly be some of the most important in all of world history.

Historians will often look at people of history and try to compare them with each other trying to find out who has played the largest role in preserving the faith. In your essay, defend or reject the statement "Moses is the most important person in Jewish history of the Old Testament." Give at least two reasons for your answer.

This essay has six assignments:

Assignment	Due Date		Due Date
1. Prewriting Activities	_____	4. Works Cited	_____
2. Thesis Statement	_____	5. Rough Draft	_____
3. Outline	_____	6. Final	_____

Prewriting Activities for Essay #4
A. Ruth, Naomi, Yochanan ben Zaccai

Students of ancient Hebrews typically will spend much time studying King Solomon, King Saul, King David, Abraham, Sarah, and Moses. However, Ruth, Naomi, and Yochanan ben Zaccai are also important Hebrew figures. Read these brief summaries and answer the questions below.

Ruth and Naomi

Ruth was an ancient Moabite. Moabs were enemies of the ancient Hebrews. Ruth lived in Moab territory and married a Jew. After her husband's death, she converted to Judaism. Naomi, Ruth's mother-in-law, was living in Moab territory but decided to return to Israel after her son died.

Naomi told Ruth to stay with her people, the Moabs. Ruth replied, "Wherever you go, I will go. Wherever you lodge, I will lodge…Where you die, I will die." (Ruth 1:16) In Jerusalem Naomi arranged for Ruth to marry, and a descendant of Ruth was King David.

Yochanan ben Zaccai

When Romans invaded Jerusalem and began to murder all Jews and destroy the Jewish temple, Rabbi Yochanan ben Zaccai offered surrender to Roman general Vespasian, if the general would grant Zaccai one request. The rabbi said, "Give me Yavneh (a city with a great university), and all its sages (professors, philosophers, and religious leaders). Partly because of Rabbi Yochanan ben Zaccai's actions, many Jews lived through this hard time, and the Jewish faith remained alive up to today.

Questions

1. Who were Ruth and Naomi?_____

2. What is the story of these two women?_____
_____
_____

3. What do the actions of Ruth and Naomi tell you about friendship of the ancient Hebrews?_____
_____

4. How did Rabbi Yochanan ben Zeccai save many Jewish lives, and perhaps save the Jewish faith?_____
_____
_____

5. What do the actions of Rabbi Yochanan ben Zeccai tell you about the character of the ancient Hebrews?_____
_____

B. Early Hebrew Leaders

Early Hebrew leaders helped build a faith that has lasted approximately 4,000 years. What was the role of each? Was one leader more important than another? Following the directions of your teacher, research these early Hebrew leaders and decide, from your research, which one played the greatest role in the early Jewish faith.

Early Hebrew Leaders
Importance for Hebrews?
Abraham:
Moses:
King David:
King Saul:
King Solomon:
Naomi:
Ruth:
Yochanan ben Zaccai:

C. A Brief History of Early Judaism

Research key events in early Jewish history and detail who was most prominent in them. Which Jewish leaders were the most important during these key events?

Key Events for Ancient Hebrews	
Key Event	**Who? What?**
1. God reveals himself to man	1. God told Abraham to move to Canaan from Ur in about 1900 B.C. Jews, Christians, and Muslims believe Abraham and Sarah to be their ancestors.
2. Exodus: flight from Egypt	2._____ _____ _____
3. God makes a covenant with man	3._____ _____ _____
4. A Jewish kingdom begins	4._____ _____ _____
5. Temple of Jerusalem is built	5._____ _____ _____
6. Romans destroy Jerusalem	6._____ _____ _____
7. Jews disperse to the world (Diaspora)	7._____ _____

D. Class Discussion

When you share ideas with other students, your ideas may be reinforced, rejected, or slightly changed. Listening to your classmates' ideas will help you form your own judgment.

Each student must interview at least three classmates who do not sit next to one another. The answers to the following questions must be written down on a piece of paper.

1. What is your name?
2. Do you think Moses is the most important person in Jewish history of the Old Testament?
3. What two reasons do you have for thinking this?

Reflection

After you have written down all your classmates' responses, think about them and ask yourself the following questions. Write down your answers under your classmates' responses.

1. What do I think of these classmates' answers?
2. Which are the best answers to question #2 above?
3. Have I changed the way I think?
4. How have I changed the way I think?

You should now have a chance to present your ideas in a class discussion. If somebody says something with which you disagree, speak up! In your discussion, you may find out they are actually right and you are wrong. All possible viewpoints should be stated and defended out loud. Test your ideas in class.

5. Ancient Greece

Assignment: Write a one-paragraph response to the question below. In your essay, include a thesis and evidence, and explain how your evidence supports your thesis.

Ancient Greece has been called the birthplace of Western civilization, because this culture is the beginning of many ideas and practices of the Western world. Along with new ideas in art, architecture, and science, Greece developed and practiced a variety of political systems. A political system is the way a country is organized. Another way of saying this is the word "government." Ancient Greece is the birthplace of many forms of government.

In your essay, research the variety of governments in ancient Greece. After your studies, answer the question "Which government of ancient Greece was the best?" Make your answer as convincing as possible.

This essay has six assignments:

Assignment	Due Date		Due Date
1. Prewriting Activities	_____	4. Works Cited	_____
2. Thesis Statement	_____	5. Rough Draft	_____
3. Outline	_____	6. Final	_____

Prewriting Activities for Essay #5
A. Types of Government in Ancient Greece

In ancient Greece, from about 1500 B.C. to 146 B.C., Greek city-states experimented with many different types of government. In one type, one man would rule the entire city and would make every important decision. In another city a group of men would rule. And in another city many men made decisions. During these years, it seems nearly all of the world's different kinds of governments existed at one time or another.

In this activity, define the type of government that is listed. Ancient Greece practiced these different governments. After you have defined the governments, decide which government sounds best to you and explain why.

Types of Government in Ancient Greece	
Type of Government	**Define**
1. Monarchy	1. A king has ultimate power. When he dies, his son takes over.
2. Oligarchy	2. _____ _____
3. Tyranny	3. _____ _____
4. Democracy	4. _____ _____ _____

Question: Which type of government seems best to you? Why?_____
_____
_____

19

B. Voices of Ancient Greece

Read how ancient Greeks thought about the different forms of government. Think about their words. What do they say about democracy and tyranny? Pericles was a politician and Herodotus a historian.

I. Democracy
Pericles (460 B.C. - 429 B.C.): "When it is a question of settling private disputes, everyone is equal before the law; when it is a question of putting one person before another in positions of public responsibility, what counts is not membership of a particular class but the actual ability which the man possesses."*
Write this in your own words: _____   _____   _____   _____   _____

II. Tyranny
Herodotus (c. 430 B.C.): "They became decidedly the first of all. These things show that, while undergoing oppression, they let themselves be beaten, since then they worked for a master; but so soon as they got their freedom, each man was eager to do the best he could for himself."
Write this in your own words: _____   _____   _____   _____   _____

Question: Which system of government seems better, according to these two Greek authors? What reasons do they give?_____
_____
_____
_____
_____

C. Class Discussion

When you share ideas with other students, your ideas may be reinforced, rejected, or slightly changed. Listening to your classmates' ideas will help you form your own judgment.

Each student must interview at least three classmates who do not sit next to one another. The answers to the following questions must be written down on a piece of paper.

1. What is your name?
2. Which government of ancient Greece was best?
3. What two reasons do you have for thinking this?

Reflection

After you have written down all your classmates' responses, think about them and ask yourself the following questions. Write down your answers under your classmates' responses.

1. What do I think of my classmates' answers?
2. Which are the best answers to question #2 above?
3. Have I changed the way I think?
4. How have I changed the way I think?

You should now have a chance to present your ideas in a class discussion. If somebody says something with which you disagree, speak up! In your discussion, you may find out they are actually right and you are wrong. All possible viewpoints should be stated and defended out loud. Test your ideas in class.

6. Greek Literature

Ancient Greek mythology refers to all ancient Greek stories that explained how natural things worked. For Greeks this was their religion. Greeks believed there were many gods and that gods interacted with humans. For example, Greeks believed that Zeus was the leader of the gods and that he made sure humans and gods tried to be fair to each other. Greeks believed Zeus could punish humans with bolts of lightning if they had done wrong. Other gods and goddesses were in charge of other human activities, such as sports, farming, and even having children.

Ancient Greeks worshipped their gods in a variety of ways. Some people built giant temples to gods. Others slit an animal's throat and sprinkled its blood on an altar to a god. In your essay, answer the question "What were two of the most interesting acts of worship the Greeks practiced?" Describe in detail what the Greeks did in these two acts of worship. Explain why the Greeks worshipped in these ways.

This essay has six assignments:

Assignment	Due Date		Due Date
1. Prewriting Activities	_____	4. Works Cited	_____
2. Thesis Statement	_____	5. Rough Draft	_____
3. Outline	_____	6. Final	_____

Prewriting Activities for Essay #6
A. Greek Gods

In ancient Greek religion, or what we call Greek mythology, there was a long list of Greek gods. The gods were believed to have lived on top of Mount Olympus. In this activity find the responsibility or specialty of each of these Greek gods. The first few have been done for you. If your textbook does not have the answer, try an encyclopedia or a website.

The gods	Their specialty
1. Aphrodite	1. Goddess of Love
2. Ares	2. God of War
3. Circe	3. The Dread Goddess
4. Demeter	4.
5. Eos	5.
6. Erida	6.
7. Hades	7.
8. Hephaistos	8.
9. Hermes	9.
10. Kronos	10.
11. Pan	11.
12. Thanatos	12.
13. Zeus	13.

Question: If you were going to fight in a war as an ancient Greek soldier, to which god might you pray and what might you offer up as a sacrifice? Why? _____
_____
_____
_____
_____

B. The Worship of the Greek Gods

Ancient Greeks loved and respected their gods in a variety of ways. Research how ancient Greeks worshipped their gods.

Ancient Greeks Worshipped Gods	
Practice of the Greeks	**God Worshipped**
1. Greeks built a giant temple on Delos	1. Apollo
2. Olympic games	2. Zeus
3. Made animal sacrifices	3. Many gods
4.	4.
5.	5.
6.	6.
7.	7.
8.	8.
9.	9.
10.	10.

Questions:
1. Which of these practices do you think is the most interesting? Why?_____ _____ _____ _____
2. How do some people today worship? _____ _____ _____
3. In what ways are religious practices today similar to or different from the worship of the ancient Greeks?_____ _____ _____ _____

C. Class Discussion

When you share ideas with other students, your ideas may be reinforced, rejected, or slightly changed. Listening to your classmates' ideas will help you form your own judgment.

Each student must interview at least three classmates who do not sit next to one another. The answers to the following questions must be written down on a piece of paper.

1. What is your name?
2. What were two of the most interesting acts of worship the Greeks practiced?
3. What two reasons do you have for thinking this?

Reflection

After you have written down all your classmates' responses, think about them and ask yourself the following questions. Write down your answers under your classmates' responses.

1. What do I think of my classmates' answers?
2. Which are the best answers to question #2 above?
3. Have I changed the way I think?
4. How have I changed the way I think?

You should now have a chance to present your ideas in a class discussion. If somebody says something with which you disagree, speak up! In your discussion, you may find out they are actually right and you are wrong. All possible viewpoints should be stated and defended out loud. Test your ideas in class.

7. Ancient India

In about 1500 B.C. Aryans invaded the Indus Valley and took over much of northern India. The Aryans, a group of warriors and herders, brought with them their way of religion, language, and political culture. The Aryans believed in many gods and had a book of religious writings called <u>The Upanishads</u>. Aryans spoke a language called Sanskrit. In addition, the Aryans had a political and social way of life called the caste system.

The Aryans were so successful in their invasion and conquering of India that many aspects of their way of life stayed in India until the 1950s. This is truly amazing! For about 3,500 years India had the caste system that the Aryans had brought with them. In your essay, answer the question "Do you think that the caste system was fair to everyone in society? Why or why not?" In your answer, make sure you describe the caste system in detail.

This essay has six assignments:

Assignment	Due Date		Due Date
1. Prewriting Activities	_____	4. Works Cited	_____
2. Thesis Statement	_____	5. Rough Draft	_____
3. Outline	_____	6. Final	_____

Prewriting Activities for Essay #7
A. What is the Caste System?

In this activity you will research what a caste system is. A caste system was a way in India that society was organized. As you find out details of the caste system, ask yourself these questions: What do I think of the caste system? Would I like to live in a place with a caste system? Why or why not?

The Caste System	
Class	**Role in Society?**
1. Brahmins, or priests	1. Provide spiritual leadership
2. Rulers and warriors	2. _____
3. _____	3. _____
4. _____	4. _____

Below the Caste System
1. In ancient India there was one group below this caste system. Which group was so low it wasn't part of the caste system?_____
2. What was its role in society?_____
3. How could a person move up or down to a different class? _____

Questions
1. What do I think of the caste system? _____
2. Would I like to live in a place with a caste system? Why or why not?_____ _____
3. When and how did the caste system officially end in India?_____

B. Class Discussion

When you share ideas with other students, your ideas may be reinforced, rejected, or slightly changed. Listening to your classmates' ideas will help you form your own judgment.

Each student must interview at least three classmates who do not sit next to one another. The answers to the following questions must be written down on a piece of paper.

1. What is your name?
2. What do you think of the caste system?
3. What two reasons do you have for thinking this?

Reflection

After you have written down all your classmates' responses, think about them and ask yourself the following questions. Write down your answers under your classmates' responses.

1. What do I think of my classmates' answers?
2. Which are the best answers to question #2 above?
3. Have I changed the way I think?
4. How have I changed the way I think?

You should now have a chance to present your ideas in a class discussion. If somebody says something with which you disagree, speak up! In your discussion, you may find out they are actually right and you are wrong. All possible viewpoints should be stated and defended out loud. Test your ideas in class.

8. Hinduism and Buddhism

Two of the world's great religions have their birthplace in India. Buddhism and Hinduism are religions professed by many people of Asia and around the world today. Originating approximately 2500 years ago, these religions share some characteristics.

Research the basic beliefs and practices of Buddhism and Hinduism. Learn how these two religions are similar and how they are different. In a well-developed essay, compare and contrast Hinduism and Buddhism. Show two ways that these religions are similar and two ways they are different.

This essay has six assignments:

Assignment	Due Date		Due Date
1. Prewriting Activities	_____	4. Works Cited	_____
2. Thesis Statement	_____	5. Rough Draft	_____
3. Outline	_____	6. Final	_____

Prewriting Activities for Essay #8
A. Hinduism

In this activity you will research the basic facts and beliefs of Hindus. Using your textbook or readings provided by your teacher answer the questions below.

Hinduism
1. When did Hinduism begin?_____
2. What is the name of the main book Hindus read for religious instruction?_____ _____
3. What is dharma?_____
4. What is karma?_____
5. Did ancient Hindus believe in the caste system?_____
6. Do Hindus believe in reincarnation (dying, and then being born into the world again)? _ _____
7. Do Hindus believe in one god, more than one god, or any god?_____ _____
8. What is the goal of someone who is a Hindu?_____ _____
9. How does a Hindu reach this goal?_____ _____
10. What is your opinion of Hinduism?_____ _____

B. Buddhism

In this activity you will research the basic facts and beliefs of Buddhists. Answer the questions below using your textbook or readings provided by your teacher.

Buddhism
1. When did Buddhism begin?_____
2. How did Buddhism begin?_____ _____
3. What means the term "the Buddha?"_____ _____
4. What are the Four Noble Truths, according to Gautama Buddha?_____ _____ _____ _____
5. What is the Middle Way?_____ _____
6. Do Buddhists believe in reincarnation (dying, and then being born into the world again)?_____
7. Do Buddhists believe in one god, more than one god, or any god?_____ _____
8. What is the goal of someone who is a Buddhist?_____ _____
9. How does a Buddhist reach this goal?_____ _____ _____
10. What is your opinion of Buddhism?_____ _____

C. Compare and Contrast

To **compare** means to look at two or more objects and recognize what they have in common. To **contrast** means to look at two or more objects and recognize what they have different from each other.

Compare and contrast Buddhism with Hinduism.

BUDDHISM AND HINDUISM		
Buddhism		**Hinduism**
Differences	Similarities	Differences
1. Nirvana	1. reincarnation	1. continual reincarnation
2.	2.	2.
3.	3.	3.
4.	4.	4.
5.	5.	5.

D. Class Discussion

When you share ideas with other students, your ideas may be reinforced, rejected, or slightly changed. Listening to your classmates' ideas will help you form your own judgment.

Each student must interview at least three classmates who do not sit next to one another. The answers to the following questions must be written down on a piece of paper.

1. What is your name?
2. In which two ways are Hinduism and Buddhism similar and different?
3. What two reasons do you have for thinking this?

Reflection

After you have written down all your classmates' responses, think about them and ask yourself the following questions. Write down your answers under your classmates' responses.

1. What do I think of my classmates' answers?
2. Which are the best answers to question #2 above?
3. Have I changed the way I think?
4. How have I changed the way I think?

You should now have a chance to present your ideas in a class discussion. If somebody says something with which you disagree, speak up! In your discussion, you may find out they are actually right and you are wrong. All possible viewpoints should be stated and defended out loud. Test your ideas in class.

9. Ancient China

China has one of the world's oldest civilizations, beginning about 4,500 years ago. As in all early civilizations, geography was a key factor as to where the first settlements began. The first Chinese societies started near the rivers of the Yellow, the Yangtze, and the Hsi. These early societies would later develop into the great Chinese dynasties.

One of the greatest tasks Chinese leaders had was in unifying all the Chinese in one government. In your essay, answer the question "What made unifying ancient China so difficult?"

This essay has six assignments:

Assignment	Due Date		Due Date
1. Prewriting Activities	_____	4. Works Cited	_____
2. Thesis Statement	_____	5. Rough Draft	_____
3. Outline	_____	6. Final	_____

Prewriting Activities for Essay #9
A. Calligraphy

Calligraphy is a Chinese way of writing. Instead of letters, which represent sound, in calligraphy small pictures represent whole words and ideas. Calligraphy was introduced to ancient China in the Shang period, over 3,500 years ago. Before calligraphy, Chinese could not communicate well with each other throughout all of China.

Written language was very important to China, as it made it possible for all Chinese people to communicate with each other. In ancient China, each Chinese settlement had a different way of speaking the Chinese language. These differences, called dialects, made it hard for people from different cities and villages to communicate with each other. Since calligraphy had pictures, which represented whole words or ideas, all Chinese could communicate with this new written language.

Chinese Writing – Calligraphy

Research calligraphy. Try to draw Chinese symbols in the boxes below. Write underneath what your symbol represents.

35

B. Geography of China

Take out a map of China, which shows deserts, mountains, and rivers. Imagine you are a very powerful and aggressive military leader who lived 4,000 years ago in China. Answer the following questions about the geography of China. After you have answered the questions, try to imagine yourself setting out with a strong army in ancient China to unify the country. What would be the most challenging aspect to unify China?

Questions:

1. By looking at a map, how would you describe China?_____
_____

2. What mountain range is to the southwest of China?_____
_____

3. Where is the largest mountain in the world located and what is its name?_____
_____
_____

4. What mountain range is to the north of China?_____
_____

5. What desert is to the northwest of China?_____
_____

6. Name the major rivers of China and describe where they are._____
_____
_____

7. Are there mountains all throughout China?_____
_____

8. Would mountains make it difficult to conquer a country? Why or why not?_____
_____

9. Would rivers make it difficult to travel in ancient China? Why or why not?_____
_____

10. What do you think might be the most challenging part of unifying ancient China?
_____
_____

C. Class Discussion

When you share ideas with other students, your ideas may be reinforced, rejected, or slightly changed. Listening to your classmates' ideas will help you form your own judgment.

Each student must interview at least three classmates who do not sit next to one another. The answers to the following questions must be written down on a piece of paper.

1. What is your name?
2. What made unifying ancient China so difficult?
3. What two reasons do you have for thinking this?

Reflection

After you have written down all your classmates' responses, think about them and ask yourself the following questions. Write down your answers under your classmates' responses.

1. What do I think of my classmates' answers?
2. Which are the best answers to question #2 above?
3. Have I changed the way I think?
4. How have I changed the way I think?

You should now have a chance to present your ideas in a class discussion. If somebody says something with which you disagree, speak up! In your discussion, you may find out they are actually right and you are wrong. All possible viewpoints should be stated and defended out loud. Test your ideas in class.

10. Confucianism

Ancient China was arguably the world's most advanced civilization. Possibly the greatest philosophers of China lived in the fifth and sixth centuries B.C. Philosophers of ancient China taught that people should respect peace, honor families, be dutiful, and have good behavior. Two such philosophers were Confucius and Lao-tzu. This essay will focus on Confucius.

Confucius (551-479 B.C.) is sometimes called China's first philosopher and first teacher. The time in which Confucius lived was marked by much violence between kings and nobles. Confucius taught his students through short sayings how to have a peaceful society. After he died his students wrote these sayings down in a book that is called Lunyu in Chinese and The Analects in English.

Read a small collection of Confucius' sayings on the following page. After reading, answer the following question. "For a society to be strong and peaceful, which two of these sayings do you think are most important?" Paraphrase these two sayings and explain why you think a society should follow these ideas.

This essay has six assignments:

Assignment	Due Date		Due Date
1. Prewriting Activities	_____	4. Works Cited	_____
2. Thesis Statement	_____	5. Rough Draft	_____
3. Outline	_____	6. Final	_____

Prewriting Activities for Essay #10
A. Paraphrase Writings of Confucius

Paraphrase the following quotations by Confucius. On your own, research more words of Confucius.

1. "Before you embark on a journey of revenge, dig two graves."
Paraphrase: _____
_____

2. "Forget injuries. Never forgive kindnesses."
Paraphrase: _____
_____

3. "He who will not economize will have to agonize."
Paraphrase: _____
_____

4. "The superior man, when resting in safety, does not forget that danger may come. When in a state of security he does not forget the possibility of ruin."
Paraphrase: _____
_____

5. "When anger rises, think of the consequences."
Paraphrase: _____
_____

6. "I am not one who was born in the possession of knowledge; I am one who is fond of antiquity, and earnest in seeking it there."
Paraphrase: _____
_____

7. "Hold faithfulness and sincerity as first principles."
Paraphrase: _____
_____

8. "If a man withdraws his mind from the love of beauty, and applies it as sincerely to the love of the virtuous; if, in serving his parents, he can exert his utmost strength; if, in serving his prince, he can devote his life; if in his intercourse with his friends, his words are sincere - although men say that he has not learned, I will certainly say that he has."
Paraphrase: _____
_____

B. Most Important Sayings

Rate the importance of the quotes on the preceding page for a society to be strong and peaceful and explain why you gave the verses this rating. A rating of 1 means "most important."

Quote #	Rating (1-4)	Reason for this Rating

Quote #	Rating (1-4)	Reason for this Rating

Quote #	Rating (1-4)	Reason for this Rating

Quote #	Rating (1-4)	Reason for this Rating

C. Class Discussion

When you share ideas with other students, your ideas may be reinforced, rejected, or slightly changed. Listening to your classmates' ideas will help you form your own judgment.

Each student must interview at least three classmates who do not sit next to one another. The answers to the following questions must be written down on a piece of paper.

1. What is your name?
2. Which two of Confucius' sayings do you think are the most important for a society to follow to be strong and peaceful?
3. Why do you think this?

Reflection

After you have written down all your classmates' responses, think about them and ask yourself the following questions. Write down your answers under your classmates' responses.

1. What do I think of my classmates' answers?
2. Which are the best answers to question #2 above?
3. Have I changed the way I think?
4. How have I changed the way I think?

You should now have a chance to present your ideas in a class discussion. If somebody says something with which you disagree, speak up! In your discussion, you may find out they are actually right and you are wrong. All possible viewpoints should be stated and defended out loud. Test your ideas in class.

11. The Roman Republic

Not enough can be said of the Roman Republic, which existed from 509 B.C. to 60 B.C. Its government was the model American Founders used to create the United States of America in 1789. Roman laws became the framework of legal systems in many countries, such as France, Great Britain, Spain, and the United States of America. The language of Rome is the ancestor of all romance languages, such as Portuguese, Spanish, French, and Romanian. Roman architectural structures are still in use today. Without a doubt, understanding the Roman Republic is essential to understanding Western civilization.

While there is no debate about the greatness of the Roman Republic, there are questions of what led to the success. Was it the government, the laws, the architecture, the army? In your essay, answer the questions "What are the two most important causes of the greatness of the Roman Republic? What allowed the Roman Republic to be a success for over 440 years?"

In your answer, know these terms as they relate to the Roman Empire:

Republic	Romulus and Remus	architecture
tribunes	veto	branches of government
Twelve Tables	Cincinnatus	written constitution
Roman Law	dictator	Roman army

This essay has six assignments:

Assignment	Due Date		Due Date
1. Prewriting Activities	_____	4. Works Cited	_____
2. Thesis Statement	_____	5. Rough Draft	_____
3. Outline	_____	6. Final	_____

Prewriting Activities for Essay #11
A. Taking Notes

Following the structure below, write notes. Research as many terms as your teacher requires.

Republic

What?_____

Who?_____

When?_____

Where?_____

Why?_____

Did this term cause the Roman Republic to be great? How? _____

_____

_____

_____

Romulus and Remus

What?_____

Who?_____

When?_____

Where?_____

Why?_____

Did this term cause the Roman Republic to be great? How? _____

_____

_____

_____

B. Republic

A **government** is a group of people who lead a country. In the Roman Republic, the government was a republic. A **republic** is a government where citizens vote for representatives who govern. Founders of the United States of America looked to the ancient Romans for ideas on how to govern. From 1775-1789, Thomas Jefferson, Benjamin Franklin, John Adams, James Madison, George Washington and others formed our government. These men did not want to have a king, but they could not find an example of a government in the world where there wasn't a king or a dictator. American Founding Fathers looked back over 2,000 years to the Roman Republic for ideas. Because of this, the government of the United States looks very much the same as the government of the Roman Republic.

In this activity, research how the government of the Roman Republic was formed, and notice how similar it is to the government of the United States of America.

Government of the United States of America		
1. Congress	**2. President**	**3. Courts (Judges)**
Makes the law	Enforces the law	Interpret the law

Who chooses leaders of government in the U.S.A.? <u>Citizens of the U.S.A.</u>

Government of the Roman Republic		
1. _____	**2.** _____	**3.** _____(Judges)
Makes the law	Enforces the law	Interprets the law

Who chose leaders of government in the Roman Republic? _____

Questions: Fill in the blanks above with answers to these questions.
1. Who made law in the Roman Republic?
2. Who enforced the law in the Roman Republic?
3. Who interpreted the law in the Roman Republic?
(interpret means to say if the law is fair or not)
4. Who chose leaders of government in the Roman Republic?
5. How is the American government similar to the Roman government? _____

C. Class Discussion

When you share ideas with other students, your ideas may be reinforced, rejected, or slightly changed. Listening to your classmates' ideas will help you form your own judgment.

Each student must interview at least three classmates who do not sit next to one another. The answers to the following questions must be written down on a piece of paper.

1. What is your name?
2. What are the two most important causes of the greatness of the Roman Republic?
3. Why do you think this?

Reflection

After you have written down all your classmates' responses, think about them and ask yourself the following questions. Write down your answers under your classmates' responses.

1. What do I think of my classmates' answers?
2. Which are the best answers to question #2 above?
3. Have I changed the way I think?
4. How have I changed the way I think?

You should now have a chance to present your ideas in a class discussion. If somebody says something with which you disagree, speak up! In your discussion, you may find out they are actually right and you are wrong. All possible viewpoints should be stated and defended out loud. Test your ideas in class.

12. Christianity

The birth of Jesus Christ in an animal stable over 2,000 years ago heralded the beginning of the world's largest religious belief, Christianity. Approximately 33 years after this birth, the Roman governor in Palestine Pontius Pilate ordered this man to be put to death on a cross. From such small beginnings started the religious belief with over two billion believers in our present day.

From its beginning, Christianity has been a persecuted religion. Followers of Christ were tortured and fed to gladiatorial animals in the Roman circus by the Roman Emperors. However, as time went on, the relationship between the Christian Church and the Roman Empire changed.

In your essay, answer the question "Why did the Roman Empire change from persecuting Christians at the time of the death of Jesus to supporting Christians by the Fourth Century?"

In your answer, you should be familiar with these terms:

Messiah	Jesus Christ	New Testament	St. Paul	St. Peter
Apostle	Trinity	resurrection	salvation	Pope
Constantine	Theodosius	missionary	Gentile	

This essay has six assignments:

Assignment	Due Date		Due Date
1. Prewriting Activities	_____	4. Works Cited	_____
2. Thesis Statement	_____	5. Rough Draft	_____
3. Outline	_____	6. Final	_____

Prewriting Activities for Essay #12
A. Taking Notes

Following the structure below, write notes. Research as many terms as your teacher requires. Keep in mind you have to use five or more sources in your essay.

Messiah

What?_____

Who?_____

When?_____

Where?_____

Why?_____

Did this term change the way the Roman Empire got along with the Christian Church?___

_____

_____

Jesus Christ

What?_____

Who?_____

When?_____

Where?_____

Why?_____

Did this term change the way the Roman Empire got along with the Christian Church?___

_____

_____

B. What is Christianity?

In this activity you will research the basic facts and beliefs of Christians. Using your textbook or readings provided by your teacher answer these questions.

Christianity
1. When did Christianity begin?_____
2. How did Christianity begin?_____ _____
3. What does it mean to be a Christian?_____ _____
4. What is the primary book for Christians?_____ _____ _____
5. What did the Old Testament say about a Messiah?_____ _____
6. For a Christian, what does salvation mean?_____
7. Who is Saint Peter?_____ _____
8. Who is Saint Paul and what did he do?_____ _____
9. How did Christianity spread throughout the Roman Empire?_____ _____ _____
10. What is your opinion of Christianity?_____ _____

Paraphrase: Here is a quote from Jesus in the New Testament (John 15:13) "No one can have greater love than to lay down his life for his friends."   In your own words, write what Jesus said: _____ _____ _____

C. Change over Time

Change over time refers to the idea that people, countries, groups, knowledge, and just about everything change over time. As students of history we should be aware of this idea of change. We should be able to analyze these changes and decide how the changes affect people. Just think how much the invention of the car changed how people travel. Similarly, imagine a life where our society would still have slavery. To understand change in societies is important as a historian.

For this exercise, research and write how the relationship of the Roman Empire with Christianity changed from the death of Jesus to the year A.D. 395.

Questions

1. Who was Saul of Tarsus, and how did he change his mind about Christians?_____
_____
_____

2. What did Saint Paul do to spread Christianity? _____
_____

3. According to tradition, how did Saint Peter and Saint Paul die? _____
_____
_____

4. What did the Roman Emperor Nero (A.D. 64) do to Christians when he believed Christians had set fire to Rome? _____
_____

5. What did the Roman Emperor Decius (A.D. 250) order his soldiers to do to Christians who refused to worship Roman gods?_____
_____

6. What did Emperor Constantine do in A.D. 313 that was good for Christians?_____
_____
_____

7. What did Emperor Theodosius declare in A.D. 395 regarding the Christian faith? _____
_____
_____

D. Class Discussion

When you share ideas with other students, your ideas may be reinforced, rejected, or slightly changed. Listening to your classmates' ideas will help you form your own judgment.

Each student must interview at least three classmates who do not sit next to one another. The answers to the following questions must be written down on a piece of paper.

1. What is your name?
2. What caused the Roman Empire to change from persecuting Christians to supporting them?
3. What evidence do you have that supports what you think?

Reflection

After you have written down all your classmates' responses, think about them and ask yourself the following questions. Write down your answers under your classmates' responses.

1. What do I think of my classmates' answers?
2. Which are the best three answers to question #2 above?
3. Have I changed the way I think?
4. How have I changed the way I think?

You should now have a chance to present your ideas in a class discussion. If somebody says something with which you disagree, speak up! In your discussion, you may find out they are actually right and you are wrong. All possible viewpoints should be stated and defended out loud. Test your ideas in class.

Part Two: Social Studies Literacy Curriculum

Chapter III: Skills for the One-Paragraph Essay

1. Fact or Opinion?

Fact

A **fact** in history is a statement that is accepted as true and is not debatable. A fact often refers to a date, a person, or a document. For example, "The Declaration of Independence was written and signed in 1776." We know this happened because we have the original document, the men who wrote and signed this document wrote about it, and observers wrote about it as well. There is no doubt in anybody's mind whether the facts in this statement are true.

Which of these sentences are facts and which are not?

Fact or Not a Fact?
1. _____ The first Egyptian settlements were near the Euphrates River.
2. _____ Early civilizations often settled near major rivers.
3. _____ Another way of saying Old Stone Age is Paleolithic.
4. _____ Early man used guns to hunt buffaloes.
5. _____ California has the best waves to surf in the United States.

Opinion

An **opinion** is an expression of somebody's ideas and is debatable. Opinions that are based on facts and good reasoning are stronger than opinions not based on facts. In history, opinions alone tend to be less persuasive than when a person supports his opinions with facts.

Are the following opinions or facts?

Opinion or Fact?
1. _____ Life for early man was more peaceful than our life today.
2. _____ Teachers who are nice don't assign homework.
3. _____ Almost everybody's favorite food is pizza.
4. _____ Mesopotamia means "the land between two rivers."
5. _____ Sumerians were the first people to use wheeled vehicles.

Now that you've learned the difference between fact and opinion, read the example paragraphs below and answer the questions. These two students attempted to answer the question "Did the ancient civilizations of Mesopotamia contribute much to world civilizations?"

Student 1: The ancient civilizations of Mesopotamia contributed much to the world. These societies rocked! When there was a really big war, the Sumerians and Assyrians knew how to fight hard. These societies would use a lot of arrows in their battles, and the enemy wouldn't know how to respond. Most of the time, the enemy would just die, or quit. Also, everyone knows that Mesopotamia had the best kind of clothing. Have you seen pictures of the great Babylonian kings? Their clothing was "tight." And, Mesopotamia was the land between two rivers, so therefore this area had to have a lot of water. All in all, the ancient civilizations of Mesopotamia contributed much to the world.

Student 2: The ancient civilizations of Mesopotamia contributed much to the world. The Sumerians created the first written language. We call this "Cuneiform." Sumerians also were the first people to use the wheel for transportation. The Babylonian king Hammurabi established one of the first written law codes, known as Hammurabi's Code. These laws helped the weak against the strong, protected women's property rights, and regulated doctors' fees. Also, the Hittites discovered how to use iron, which at that time was the strongest metal in the world that humans could work with. Phoenicians gave us the world's first alphabet, with 22 symbols. In addition, the Hebrews were the first people ever to worship only one God. Yes, the ancient civilizations of Mesopotamia contributed much to the world.

Questions
1. Which of these two students uses more opinion than fact? _____
2. Copy one sentence that is an opinion. _____
3. Copy one sentence that details at least one fact._____
4. Which of these two students' writings is more persuasive? Why? _____

2. Judgment

Judgment in social studies means a person's evaluation of facts. For example, if we use the fact that the Romans believed citizens could vote, we can judge from this that the Romans looked somewhat favorably on democracy. Good judgment is very persuasive but bad judgment is not.

Write facts and judgments in the spaces provided. Discuss your judgments in class.

Fact: 11-year-old Maria Perez won the gold medal in the city 800-meter sprint.
Judgment: Maria is a fast runner.

Fact: Private Smith was killed in war and had one wife and 7 children.
Judgment: Private Smith's death was a tragedy.

Fact: Thursday's temperature in Santa Ana was 105 degrees Fahrenheit.
Judgment: Thursday was very hot.

Make your own.

Fact:
Judgment:

Fact:
Judgment:

Fact:
Judgment:

3. Supporting Evidence

Supporting evidence refers to everything you use to support your thesis. These include, but are not limited to, the following.

1. Diaries and journals
2. Government documents such as birth certificates
3. Songs and stories
4. Coins, medals, jewelry
5. Artistic works such as pictures and paintings
6. Tools and pottery
7. Documents such as the Declaration of Independence
8. Weapons
9. Burial remains
10. Literature and customs

Good writers overwhelm the reader with so many pieces of supporting evidence that the writing will be quickly accepted. Also, the writer has a duty to explain carefully and logically the meaning of the evidence, showing how it supports the thesis. A writer must be careful, however, not to include unnecessary evidence. For example, the fact that Lincoln was born in a log cabin isn't evidence that he was a good president. Also, the dates a president was born and died may be evidence, but they would not support a thesis arguing who was the best president.

Practice

With your teacher discuss which of the following is evidence for the topic "Explain what daily life was like in the Roman Republic in the third century B.C."
1. A diary from 234 B.C.
2. A newspaper article from A.D. 250
3. Your friend likes the subject
4. A movie about life in the third century B.C.
5. A song Romans sang in the third century B.C.
6. A story on the crucifixion of Christ
7. A painting of a Roman slave working in 299 A.D.

4. Primary or Secondary Source Analysis

A **primary source** is a piece of evidence authored by a person who witnessed or experienced a historical event. For example, diaries and journals are primary sources. It is usually better to find out something from a person who experienced a particular event than to hear about it secondhand. Primary source documents are usually the most useful for historians.

A **secondary source** is a piece of evidence that has been worked on by somebody who was not a witness to the historical event. Examples of secondary sources are textbooks, documentaries, and encyclopedias. Secondary sources are valuable but not as valuable as primary sources. Secondary sources contain the bias of the writer. This means that the writer of a secondary source will put his ideas into his explanation of the historical event, even when he may be trying not to.

       Take a look at these two examples regarding the same event.
       Event: Car accident outside of school

Example 1: "Oh no! I was in the back seat of my mom's car. This kid threw his friend's handball onto the street. All of a sudden, his friend jumped in front of my mom's car to get his ball. He didn't even look if a car was coming. My mom hit him and his body smashed against our windshield. Blood was everywhere!"

Example 2: "Did you hear what happened? Mario told me that his brother was walking home when he dropped his handball onto the street. After his brother looked both ways for cars, he stepped out onto the street to get his ball. Then this mad lady came speeding down the street and aimed her car at him. She hit him on purpose!"

Questions
1. Which is a primary source?
2. Which is a secondary source?
3. What is usually more believable, a primary or secondary source? Why? _____
_____

5. Using Quotes

A **quote** is when a writer uses the exact words of another writer. An effective analytical essay in social studies will use quotes. For example, an essay about the use of violence in the Middle Ages will be stronger if certain quotes from this time period are used. When you argue a point about the past, there is no better evidence than a primary source document or quote.

Look at the example below. The paragraph is part of an answer to the question "Was the plague a problem in ancient Greece?"

The plague was most certainly a problem to the ancient Greeks. The Greek historian Thucydides, in "The Peloponnesian Wars," wrote, "Words indeed fail one when one tries to give a general picture of this disease; and as for the sufferings of individuals, they seemed almost beyond the capacity of human nature to endure." To the ancient Greeks, the plague was a serious problem.

When using quotes, write the original author's name and the speech or document from which the quote was taken from. Punctuate correctly with quotation marks.

Practice

Practice writing three quotations taken from your textbook. Use correct punctuation! Pay attention to the commas, the quotation marks, and the end marks.

1. _____

_____

2. _____

_____

3. _____

_____

---

6. Paraphrasing

Paraphrasing means to take information from your research and to put it in your own words. This is an important skill to have when writing a research paper. If you copy directly from a source, such as a book, but do not place the words in quotation marks and write the author's name, it is called **plagiarism**. Plagiarism is against the rules of writing and your teacher will not accept the work!

Here is an example of paraphrasing a quote from a teacher.

Quote:
"China's mountainous geography made it very difficult for Chinese leaders to unify their country."
Paraphrase:
Ancient Chinese leaders had a hard time unifying their country because of the many mountains in China.

Practice
Quote:
"Confucius lived in a time of turmoil in China. He wrote about respecting parents and authority. Many Chinese grew to believe in what Confucius wrote about."
Paraphrase:
_____
_____
_____
_____

Quote:
"The Chinese were great traders with other cultures. The Silk Road ran from China through central Asia to the Middle East. Along this trail, Chinese met with Arabs, Africans, Europeans, and other Asians."
Paraphrase:
_____
_____
_____
_____

---

7. Thesis Statement

The **thesis statement** is the main idea or argument of your entire essay. It is your main judgment regarding the essay question and it should contain words used in the prompt. A thesis statement is not a fact. Instead, it is your judgment of the facts. Because of this, a thesis has to be something with which not everyone will agree. Every thesis will provide pieces of evidence in order to provide the reader with a general outline of your essay.

Here is an example from essay question #1 in this book, "What allowed humans to change from being nomads to having permanent homes? Choose two causes that you consider most important." Defend your answer with supporting evidence.

Example 1: "The two most important causes that allowed humans to change from a nomadic lifestyle to having permanent homes were climate and inventions."

This thesis answers the question and provides an outline for the rest of the essay. The writer addresses the question directly and provides general reasons to support his answer. In the essay the writer will expand on these reasons.

Create two more examples of a thesis based on this first question.

Example 2:_____	
_____	
Example 3:_____	
_____	

The Good Thesis Test
If you can answer, "Yes," to these questions, you most likely have a good thesis for your essay:

1. Does the thesis address the prompt directly?
2. Does the thesis take a position that I can argue with evidence?
3. Could somebody argue against my thesis statement?

8. Conclusion

The **conclusion** ties the evidence presented in the essay back to the thesis statement. It is the writer's last chance to present how the evidence supports the thesis statement. In a one-paragraph essay the conclusion can be one sentence, but it may be more.

Here is an example regarding the question "What were the two most important Roman contributions to world civilizations?"

The two most important Roman contributions to world civilizations were language and law. The language of the Romans, Latin, is the mother of many world languages. Spanish, French, Portuguese, and Romanian are all Latin languages. English, although a Germanic language, has many Latin roots and is influenced by Latin languages. Think of the words "surrender" and "champagne." These English words have their beginnings in Latin. Secondly, Roman law provided a terrific building block for future civilizations. The Justinian Code, created by Emperor Justin, is still in use in France today. Also, the U.S. uses many elements of Roman law, such as the concept "innocent until proven guilty." The idea that a government needs to charge somebody with a crime in order to make an arrest, called "habeas corpus," comes from Roman law. **In conclusion, Roman civilization contributed to the world its rich Latin language and Roman law. With contributions such as the words "surrender" and "champagne," and legal concepts, such as "habeas corpus" and "innocent until proven guilty," many world civilizations are better off because of the Romans.**

Bolded sentences are the conclusion.

The Good Conclusion Test
If you can answer, "Yes," to these questions, you have written a good conclusion:

1. Does the conclusion restate the thesis?
2. Does the conclusion include pieces of evidence in my essay?
3. Does the conclusion convince the reader that the thesis is correct?

9. Outline for a One-Paragraph Essay

An outline helps you organize your thoughts and shows if you have enough evidence to support your thesis statement. An outline does not need to be written in complete sentences, except for the thesis statement and the conclusion. In a one-paragraph essay, the more evidence you include, the stronger your argument will be.

An example outline follows to the essay question "What were the two most important Roman contributions to world civilizations?"

I. Thesis Statement:
Two most important Roman contributions to world civilizations were language and law.

II. Supporting Evidence:
      1. Latin—mother of languages—French, Portuguese, Romanian, Spanish
      2. Latin and English—"surrender," "champagne"
      3. Roman law—"innocent until proven guilty"
      4. R.L.—"habeas corpus"

III. Conclusion:
In conclusion, Roman civilization contributed to the world its rich Latin language and Roman law. With contributions such as the words "surrender" and "champagne," and with legal concepts such as "habeas corpus" and "innocent until proven guilty," many world civilizations are better off because of the Romans.

Following this page are two forms. One is a "Basic Outline Form for a Paragraph," the other an "Advanced Outline Form for a Paragraph."

Basic Outline Form for a One-Paragraph Essay

(Use complete sentences for the thesis statement and the conclusion.)

I. Thesis Statement: _____

_____

       A. Supporting Evidence_____

       B. Supporting Evidence_____

       C. Supporting Evidence_____

II. Conclusion: _____

_____

Advanced Outline Form for a One-Paragraph Essay

(Use complete sentences for the thesis statement and the conclusion.)

I. Thesis Statement: _____

_____

       A. Supporting Evidence_____

       B. Supporting Evidence_____

       C. Supporting Evidence _____

       D. Supporting Evidence _____

       E. Supporting Evidence_____

II. Conclusion: _____

_____

10. Rough Draft for a One-Paragraph Essay

The **rough draft** is the first time that you will explain all the supporting evidence that you use. To do this, take your outline and explain how your evidence supports the thesis statement.   Instead of listing your evidence, you will explain its importance. Here is an example of a rough draft of a paragraph. The sentences in bold are those that explain how your evidence supports your topic sentence.

The two most important Roman contributions to world civilizations were language and law. The language of the Romans, Latin, is the mother of many world languages. Spanish, French, Portuguese, and Romanian are all Latin languages. **Just think of it. Over 200 million people owe their language to the Romans.** English, although a Germanic language, has many Latin roots and is influenced by Latin languages. **Think of the words "surrender" and "champagne." These English words have their beginnings in Latin.**   Secondly, Roman law provided a terrific building block for future civilizations. The Justinian Code, created by Emperor Justin, is still in use in France today. Also, the U.S. uses many elements of Roman law, such as the concept "innocent until proven guilty." The idea that a government needs to charge somebody with a crime in order to make an arrest, called "habeas corpus," comes from Roman law. **"Innocent until proven guilty" and "Habeas Corpus" are two legal norms that protect the rights of citizens.** In conclusion, Roman civilization contributed to the world its rich Latin language and Roman law. With contributions such as the words "surrender" and "champagne" and legal concepts such as "habeas corpus" and "innocent until proven guilty," many world civilizations are better off because of the Romans.

Basic Rough Draft Form for a One-Paragraph Essay
(Use complete sentences.)

I. Thesis Statement: _____

_____

    A. Supporting Evidence: First of all, _____

_____

Explanation (Explain how this supports the topic sentence): _____

_____

    B. Supporting Evidence: Secondly, _____

_____

Explanation (Explain how this supports the topic sentence): _____

_____

II. Conclusion: In conclusion, _____

_____

Advanced Rough Draft Form for a One-Paragraph Essay

(Use complete sentences.)

I. Thesis Statement: _____

_____

    A. Supporting Evidence: First of all, _____

_____

Explanation (Explain how this supports the topic sentence): _____

_____

    B. Supporting Evidence: Secondly, _____

_____

Explanation (Explain how this supports the topic sentence): _____

_____

    C. Supporting Evidence: Thirdly, _____

_____

Explanation (Explain how this supports the topic sentence): _____

_____

    D. Supporting Evidence: In addition, _____

_____

Explanation (Explain how this supports the topic sentence): _____

_____

    E. Supporting Evidence: Also, _____

_____

Explanation (Explain how this supports the topic sentence): _____

_____

II. Conclusion: _____

_____

Chapter III: Skills for the Five-Paragraph Essay

11. Taking Notes

All research papers require the student to read, analyze, and write information that is helpful in answering the question asked. The structure of your note taking depends on the question. Before reading, structure your notes in a way so you will focus on important information and not on unimportant details that would take valuable time. Below is an example of a structure of notes based on the question "What led to the Cold War?" Notice that the last question helps you stick to your topic.

Socrates
What?
Who?
When?
Where?
Why?
What does the life of Socrates tell you about ancient Greece?
Source and page(s):

When taking notes be sure to list the source. You can do this quickly by writing only the last name of the author and the page on which you found the information. This will save you much time later when you are documenting the source in your essay. When you are writing your final essay you don't want to be stuck in the position of rummaging through your papers or flipping through your book, trying to find exactly from where you took your information.

12. Thesis Statement for a Five-Paragraph Essay

The **thesis statement** is the main idea or argument of your entire essay. It is your judgment regarding the essay question and it should contain words used in the prompt. A thesis statement is not a fact. Instead, it is your judgment of the evidence. Because of this, a thesis has to be something with which not everyone will agree. In a five-paragraph essay you should list three pieces of evidence in your thesis in order to provide the reader with an outline of your essay.

Here is an example from the essay question "What made unifying ancient China so difficult?" Because this essay requires a five-paragraph response, the student will need three supporting pieces of evidence for the body paragraphs. These three should be included in the thesis.

Example 1: Unifying ancient China was so difficult because of geography, language, and foreign invasions.

This thesis answers the question and provides an outline for paragraphs two, three, and four. Paragraph two will detail information about foreign policy, paragraph three about domestic affairs, and paragraph four about presidential elections.

Create two more thesis statements for a five-paragraph essay based on this question.

Example 2: _____	
_____	
Example 3: _____	

The Good Thesis Test
If you can answer, "Yes," to these questions, you most likely have a good thesis for a five-paragraph essay:

1. Does my thesis address the prompt directly?
2. Does my thesis take a position that I can argue with evidence?
3. Could somebody argue against my thesis statement?

13. The Topic Sentence and the Closer

The **topic sentence** is the main idea of a paragraph in the body of a multiple-paragraph essay. In a five-paragraph essay, a topic sentence takes one of the pieces of evidence in the thesis and states it strongly. The body of this paragraph will support the topic sentence.

Here is one example of a topic sentence for the question, "What made unifying ancient China so difficult?"
Thesis Statement: Ancient China was so difficult to unify because of geography, language, and foreign invasions.
Topic Sentence for Paragraph Two: Ancient China was so difficult to unify because of geography.

Write topic sentences for paragraphs three and four in the box below.

Paragraph Three:	_____
Paragraph Four:	_____

The Closer

The **closer** ties the evidence presented in the paragraph back to the topic sentence. It is the writer's last chance to present how the evidence supports the topic sentence before moving on. Here is an example regarding the same essay question as above. The last sentence of the following paragraph is the closer.

> Ancient China was so difficult to unify because of geography. China has many large mountain ranges. In the southwest, the Himalayas contain the largest mountain in the world, Mt. Everest, over 29,000 feet tall. Other mountain ranges include the Kunlan Shan, the Altai, and the Tian Shan. Mountains throughout China made it difficult to communicate and travel between communities. China also has huge deserts. The largest of the deserts is the Gobi Desert in the northwest. Traveling across this desert took great planning and many supplies. It was too challenging for a government to send an army across the Gobi Desert and unify all of China. In conclusion, large mountain ranges and huge deserts made it difficult for ancient China to unify.

14. Outlining a Five-Paragraph Essay

An **outline** is a skeleton for your essay. Here, you organize your essay before writing it out in complete sentences. If you have a framework first, it will be fairly easy to write the essay. Below is an explanation of writing an outline for a five-paragraph essay.

A. First Paragraph

For the first paragraph, it is enough to write down the thesis and list the three topics that will be your body paragraphs.

B. Body Paragraphs

1. Organize your paragraphs into topics by following the order you wrote in the thesis. Your thesis should have listed three topics. The first will be the topic of your second paragraph, the second the topic of your third paragraph, and the third the topic of your fourth paragraph.

2. You do not need to write complete sentences for your outline. It is enough to write the topics of each paragraph and to list the supporting evidence for your topic sentence in your outline. You will add more information when you write your draft.

3. Document each source! Write the author's last name and the page where you found this information.

C. Conclusion:

The conclusion is the place where you restate your thesis and your topic sentences. You will convince the reader better by a reminder at the end what your essay was all about. After the restatements, finish the essay with strong words supporting your thesis.

Following this page are two forms — one basic and one advanced — to help you develop your outline.

Basic Outline Form for a Five-Paragraph Essay

(Use complete sentences for the thesis, topic sentences, closers, and conclusion.)

Paragraph I.
Thesis Statement:_____

_____

Paragraph II.
I. Topic Sentence: _____

_____

      A. Supporting Evidence:_____

      B. Supporting Evidence:_____

II. Closer: _____

_____Write the source:_____

Paragraph III.
I. Topic Sentence: _____

_____

      A. Supporting Evidence:_____

      B. Supporting Evidence:_____

II. Closer: _____

_____Write the source:_____

Paragraph IV.
I. Topic Sentence: _____

_____

      A. Supporting Evidence:_____

      B. Supporting Evidence:_____

II. Closer: _____

_____Write the source:_____

Paragraph V. Conclusion
I. Restate thesis statement: _____

_____

II. Strong statement that shows how the topic sentences support the thesis:_____

_____

_____

Advanced Outline Form for a Five-Paragraph Essay

(Use complete sentences for the thesis, topic sentences, closers, and conclusion.)

Paragraph I.
Thesis Statement: _____

_____

Paragraph II.
I. Topic Sentence: _____

_____

      A. Supporting Evidence:_____

      B. Supporting Evidence: _____

      C. Supporting Evidence:_____

      D. Supporting Evidence:_____

      E. Supporting Evidence:_____

II. Closer: _____

_____Write the source:_____

Paragraph III.
I. Topic Sentence: _____

_____

      A. Supporting Evidence:_____

      B. Supporting Evidence: _____

      C. Supporting Evidence:_____

      D. Supporting Evidence:_____

      E. Supporting Evidence:_____

II. Closer: _____

_____Write the source:_____

Paragraph IV. Use another page or the back of this paper.

Paragraph V. Conclusion
I. Restate thesis statement: _____

_____

II. Strong Statement that shows how the topic sentences support the thesis:_____

_____

_____

15. Writing a Rough Draft for a Five-Paragraph Essay

A.   Introductory Paragraph

The Social Studies short essay begins directly with the thesis. Following the thesis is a brief explanation of the main topics that will be written in detail in the body paragraphs. Below is an example response to the essay question "What made unifying ancient China so difficult?"

Ancient China was so difficult to unify because of geography, language, and foreign invasions. Deserts and mountains cover China in such a way that it was difficult for ancient man to communicate and travel. Before the Zhou Dynasty, Chinese neither spoke nor wrote in a completely uniform manner. Furthermore, nomadic raiders from outside of China presented great dangers.

B.   The Body

The body of your essay is where you present your evidence to prove your thesis. In these paragraphs, you will present your evidence and explain how it supports the topic sentence. Keep the order of your arguments the same as the order of mention in the thesis. Attempt to order the events chronologically.

C.   Conclusion

In this paragraph, you need to restate your thesis, tie the topic sentences of your body paragraphs to the thesis, and leave the reader with the strongest evidence that supports your argument. Your job is to convince the reader that your position is correct. Write strongly.

Following this page are two forms — one basic and one advanced — to help you develop your rough draft.

Basic Rough Draft Form for a Five-Paragraph Essay
(Use complete sentences. Use the back when you need space.)

Paragraph I.
Thesis Statement:_____
_____

Paragraph II.
Topic Sentence: _____
_____

A. Supporting Evidence: First of all, _____
_____

Explanation (Explain how the evidence supports the thesis): _____
_____

B. Supporting Evidence: Secondly,_____
_____

Explanation (Explain how the evidence supports the thesis): _____
_____

II. Closer: In conclusion, _____
_____

Paragraphs III and IV. Follow the structure of paragraph II.

Paragraph V. Conclusion
I. Restate thesis statement: _____
_____
_____

II. Strong statement that shows how the topic sentences support the thesis: _____
_____
_____

Advanced Rough Draft Form for a Five-Paragraph Essay
(Use complete sentences.)

Paragraph I.
I. Thesis Statement: _____

_____

Paragraph II.
I. Topic Sentence: _____

A. Supporting Evidence: First of all, _____

_____

Explanation (Explain how this supports the thesis): _____

_____

B. Supporting Evidence: Secondly, _____

_____

Explanation (Explain how this supports the thesis): _____

_____

C. Supporting Evidence: Thirdly, _____

_____

Explanation (Explain how this supports the thesis): _____

_____

D. Supporting Evidence: In addition, _____

_____

Explanation (Explain how this supports the thesis): _____

_____

E. Supporting Evidence: Furthermore, _____

_____

Explanation (Explain how this supports the thesis): _____

_____

II. Closer: _____

_____

Paragraphs III and IV. Follow the same structure as above.

Paragraph V. Conclusion
I. Restate thesis statement: _____

_____

II. Strong statement that shows how the topic sentences support the thesis:

_____

_____

16. Revising

After writing the rough draft, it is necessary to revise. Revising involves four steps. Take your essay and perform these four tasks with a red pen in hand.

STEP I   Deletion

Delete	the end, every, just, nice, great, bad, got, everything, getting,
dead words:	so, well, a lot, lots, get, good, some, yours, you, your very

STEP II   Addition

A.   Add words, facts, or better descriptions. Imagine you are writing for an adult who does not know the subject well. Explain every point precisely.

B.   Use transitions whenever helpful.

To add ideas
further, furthermore, moreover, in addition

To show results
therefore, consequently, as a result

To indicate order
first, second, in addition to

To summarize
to sum up, to summarize, in short

To compare
similarly, likewise, by comparison

Conclusion
In conclusion, to conclude, finally

STEP III   Substitution

Substitute repetitive words and weak-sounding words.

A.   Underline the first word in each sentence. If the words are the same, change some of the words.

B.   Read your thesis, topic sentences, closers, and conclusion; change words as needed. Is your word choice powerful and effective? Will your essay convince the reader?

STEP IV   Rearrangement

Write sentences that have a variety of beginnings.

Adjective beginnings
Well-equipped, dedicated Union soldiers won the American Civil War.

"ing" words
Riding horses was common among most 1800s Americans.

Prepositional Phrases
Over the vast Pacific Ocean, Columbus sailed.

Dependent Clauses
Because of Lincoln, the North did not give up the war effort.

"ly" words
Bravely, Washington led the Continental Army to victory.

Adverbs
Slowly, but surely, Grant moved the Union Army

17. Documenting Sources in the Text

When you take information from a source and use it in a paragraph, you cite it at the end of the paragraph. Place in parentheses the author's name and the page number you found the information. For example, if you've found out information on ancient China from a textbook written by Robert De Gree, you would cite it as the last sentence in the example below.

Ancient China was so difficult to unify because of geography. China has many large mountain ranges. In the southwest, the Himalayas contain the largest mountain in the world, Mt. Everest, over 29,000 feet tall. Other mountain ranges include the Kunlan Shan, the Altai, and the Tian Shan. Mountains throughout China made it difficult to communicate and travel between communities. China also has huge deserts. The largest of the deserts is the Gobi Desert in the northwest. Traveling across this desert took great planning and many supplies. It was too challenging for a government to send an army across the Gobi Desert and unify all of China. In conclusion, large mountain ranges and huge deserts made it difficult for ancient China to unify. (De Gree, pages 399-450).

Note: This is according to Gibaldi, Joseph, MLA Handbook for Writers of Research Papers, (New York: The Modern Language Association of America, 1995).

18. Works Cited

At the end of your document, on a separate piece of paper, write "Works Cited" at the top middle. After this, write your sources in alphabetical order using the following format:

Book
Author (Last Name, First Name). Title of Book. Place of publication: Publisher, date. (If there is more than one author, list them in alphabetical order with a comma in between names.)

Author of one chapter in a book
Author (Last Name, First Name). "Title of chapter." Title of Book. Place of Publication: Publisher, date. Pages of chapter.

Dictionary
Title of Dictionary. Edition.

Internet
Author (if known). "Document Title." Website or Database Title. Date of electronic publication (if known). Name of sponsoring institution (if known). Date information was accessed <URL>.

Encyclopedia
"Article," Encyclopedia Title. Edition.

Interview or Lecture
Name of Speaker (Last Name, First Name). "Title of interview or lecture." Place of interview or lecture, date.

Note: This is according to Gibaldi, Joseph, MLA Handbook for Writers of Research Papers, (New York: The Modern Language Association of America, 1995).

19. Typing Guidelines

1. All final research papers must be typed. The Works Cited page must also be typed.
2. The font must be a standard typeface and style. Courier, Helvetica, and Times are good choices. Do not use italics, handwriting, or anything else decorative.
3. The size of the letters must be 12 points.
4. All margins must be one inch from the top, bottom, and each side.
5. All sentences will be double-spaced.
6. Pages will be numbered in the lower right-hand side of the page. Do not number your Cover page. The Works Cited page is numbered but does not count as a text page.

20. The Cover Page and Checklist

Cover Page

The Cover page needs to have the title of your research paper centered. It can be at the top, the middle, or the bottom of the page. You need to make an illustration by drawing in pencil, coloring in colored pencils, or using any other teacher-approved medium.

In the bottom right-hand corner, write or type your name, date, and period of your social studies teacher.

Checklist

All final papers must have these items turned in to your social studies teacher on the final due date.

Inside of a clear, plastic folder include the following items in this order:

1. Cover page   _____
2. Final draft   _____
3. Works Cited page   _____
4. Prewriting   _____
5. Outline   _____
6. Rough draft   _____

Chapter IV: Skills for the Multi-Page Essay

21. Thesis Statement for a Multi-Page Essay

As explained earlier in this book, the thesis statement is the main idea or argument of your entire essay. It is your judgment regarding the essay question and may contain the same words from the prompt. A thesis statement is not a fact. Instead, it is your judgment of the evidence. Because of this, a thesis has to be something with which not everyone will agree. In a multi-page essay, the writer need not list all the evidence he will present to support the thesis statement. However, general topics of evidence need to be presented so that the reader is aware of what the essay will entail.

A multi-page research paper represents a great deal of effort and will not be written during a timed test. Therefore, the writer may choose to write an introduction to the essay, or what some writers call a hook. Before you write the thesis, include a short, interesting introduction. (The sentence in bold is the thesis statement.)

Here is an example from the essay question "What made unifying ancient China so difficult?"

Example 1: As Chang bent to scatter the seeds into the ground, he thought of the beautiful mountains that outlined the horizon. Appreciated not only for their beauty, Chang knew his mountains also separated his village from control of the leading general and his army in China. Chang felt fortunate that his mountains gave him not only beauty but also protection. **Ancient China was difficult to unify not only because of geography, but also because of language and foreign invasions.** Deserts and mountains cover China in such a way that it was difficult for ancient man to communicate and travel. Before the Zhou Dynasty, Chinese neither spoke nor wrote in a completely uniform manner. Furthermore, nomadic raiders from outside of China presented great dangers.

The Good Thesis Test
If you can answer, "Yes," to these questions, you most likely have a good thesis for a multi-page essay:

1. Does the thesis directly address the prompt?
2. Does my thesis take a position that I can argue with evidence?
3. Could somebody argue against my thesis statement?

77

22. Counterargument

In social studies, many historians have different judgments based on the same evidence. For example, some historians view the Korean War as a success, and others view it as a great loss. These are two very different judgments on U.S. history. These two judgments can be called two **perspectives**.

When you defend your thesis statement, you should include at least one counterargument. A **counterargument** is one in which the writer presents an idea that goes against his thesis statement. Then, in that paragraph, the writer shows how this idea is wrong.

For example, imagine if the thesis statement to an essay were, "Who was the most important ancient Hebrew of the Old Testament?" The counterargument paragraph for this thesis should be at the end of the essay, perhaps right before the conclusion paragraph.

Here is an example of a counterargument paragraph:

Some historians may claim that Moses or King David is the most important Hebrew figures of the Old Testament. These historians point to the facts that Moses led the Jews out of Egyptian slavery and King David won many battles. While these accomplishments are important, these two figures are not the most important Hebrews of the Old Testament. Ruth and Naomi are. The story of Ruth and Naomi does not involve battles or killing, but it does involve friendship. Ruth and Naomi's relationship is a model for not only religious people, but for all. These two women showed that a friend is more important than a nation. They also showed that when a person makes a decision based on love and sacrifice, great events can happen. Because Ruth left her homeland to stay with Naomi, she became the ancestor of King David. In conclusion, the most important ancient Hebrews of the Old Testament are Ruth and Naomi because of their contribution to the idea of friendship and love.

Notice that the beginning of the paragraph above begins with the words "Some historians say." This is because you are presenting an idea that is opposite of yours. In your paragraph, be clear that you think these people are wrong.

23. Analyzing Primary Sources

When you read history and try to analyze it, pay attention to details of the document that tell you important details of the source. These small details can give you incredible insight as to how you should analyze the historical information. Here are a few basic questions to which you should find answers, while you are analyzing historical texts, paintings, or any historical documents.

1. Who wrote (drew, illustrated) it? What position does the writer have? Is the writer a professor, an author of novels? Is the author(s) respected in the field? Did multiple authors prepare the text?

2. Who is (was) the audience? Students? Bookstore customers? Newspaper readers? Magazine readers?

3. When was the text written (drawn/ illustrated)? Was it written during a critical time of history that the text is about? Was it written many years after the time of history it is written about? Are historians more biased about events that happen during our lifetime?

4. Who paid for the text to be written? Is there a chance that the author(s) will be biased because of who is paying for the text?

5. Where was the text written? Was the text written in a place that is in the middle of the historical study the text is about? Is it possible the author can be biased based on where it was written? What country is the author from? Is it possible the country might affect someone's perspective?

6. Who is the publisher? Could the publisher have a bias that might affect the veracity (truth) of the materials?

7. Why was the text written? What was the purpose of the text? Was it meant to be part of a textbook? Was it meant to stir emotions for or against the government?

24. Cause and Effect

Cause and effect is a term that means one event made another event happen. For example, if you push against the pedals of your bicycle, the bicycle moves. In this example, the push against the pedals is the cause and the bicycle moving is the effect.

CAUSE ------------------------------→EFFECT
push against pedals--------------→bicycle moves

In social studies, cause and effect usually relates events and people. The relationship is trickier to understand than the above example with the bicycle. Sometimes it is difficult to see causes and effects in history. Here are two examples from American history with which most historians would agree.

CAUSE --------------------------------→EFFECT
Japan attacks Pearl Harbor--------→the United States enters World War II
the U.S. drops atomic bombs on Japan -------→Japan surrenders

Now, write five causes and effects from history.

Term (Cause)   Effect
1. The North won the Civil War.   1. The U.S. did not break up in 1865.

2._____   2._____

3._____   3._____

4._____   4._____

5._____   5._____

25. Compare and Contrast

To **compare** means to look at two or more objects and recognize what they have in common. To **contrast** means to look at two or more objects and recognize what they have different from each other.

Try to compare and contrast President Reagan with President Carter.

Ronald Reagan		Jimmy Carter
Differences	**Similarities**	**Differences**
Republican	Both politicians	Democrat

81

26. Outline and Rough Draft for a Multi-Page Essay

In a longer essay, the only item that differs structurally from the smaller essays is the introductory paragraph. In smaller essays that are from one to two pages the introduction should begin with the thesis statement. In longer essays, the writer can begin with information that will catch the reader's attention and add the thesis at the end of the paragraph. Read the sample introductory paragraph below for the essay question "Why was ancient China so difficult to unify?"

As Chang bent to scatter the seeds into the ground, he thought of the beautiful mountains that outlined the horizon. Appreciated not only for their beauty, Chang knew his mountains also separated his village from control of the leading general and his army in China. Chang felt fortunate that his mountains gave him not only beauty but also protection. **Ancient China was difficult to unify not only because of geography, but also because of language and foreign invasions.** Deserts and mountains cover China in such a way that it was difficult for ancient man to communicate and travel. Before the Zhou Dynasty, Chinese neither spoke nor wrote in a completely uniform manner. Furthermore, nomadic raiders from outside of China presented great dangers.

For further help on outlining and writing a rough draft for a multi-page essay: See the following pages for outline and rough draft forms.

Basic Outline Form for a Multi-Page Essay
(Use complete sentences for thesis, topic sentences, closers, and conclusion.)

Paragraph I.
Thesis Statement: _____
_____

Paragraph II.
I. Topic Sentence: _____
_____

      A. Supporting Evidence:_____
      B. Supporting Evidence:_____
II. Closer: _____
_____Write the source:_____

Remaining Body Paragraphs.
Follow the same structure as paragraph II.

Paragraph V. Conclusion
I. Restate thesis statement: _____
_____
_____

II. Strong statement that shows how the topic sentences support the thesis:
_____
_____

Advanced Outline Form for a Multi-Page Essay
(Use complete sentences for thesis, topic sentences, closers, and conclusion.)

Paragraph I.
Thesis Statement: _____

_____

Paragraph II.
I. Topic Sentence: _____

_____

      A. Supporting Evidence: _____

      B. Supporting Evidence: _____

      C. Supporting Evidence: _____

      D. Supporting Evidence: _____

      E. Supporting Evidence: _____

II. Closer: _____

_____Write the source: _____

Remaining Body Paragraphs.
Follow the same structure as paragraph II.

Paragraph V. Conclusion
I. Restate thesis statement: _____

_____

_____

II. Strong statement that shows how the topic sentences support the thesis: _____

_____

_____

Basic Rough Draft Form for a Multi-Page Essay
(Use complete sentences. Use the back when you need space.)

Paragraph I.
Thesis Statement: _____
_____

Paragraph II.
I. Topic Sentence: _____
_____

      A. Supporting Evidence: First of all, _____
_____

Explanation (Explain how this supports the topic sentence):_____
_____

      B. Supporting Evidence: Secondly, _____
_____

Explanation (Explain how this supports the topic sentence): _____
_____

II. Closer: Show how A and B support the topic sentence. In conclusion, _____
_____

Write the source: _____

Remaining Body Paragraphs.
Follow the same structure as paragraph II.

Paragraph V. Conclusion
I. Restate thesis statement: _____
_____

II. Strong statement that shows how the topic sentences support the thesis: _____
_____
_____

Advanced Rough Draft Form for a Multi-Page Essay

(Use complete sentences. Use the back when you need space.)

Paragraph I.
Thesis Statement: _____
_____

Paragraph II.
I. Topic Sentence: _____
_____

    A. Supporting Evidence: _____
_____

Explanation (Explain how this supports the topic sentence): _____
_____

    B. Supporting Evidence: _____
_____

Explanation (Explain how this supports the topic sentence): _____
_____

    C. Supporting Evidence: _____
_____

Explanation (Explain how this supports the topic sentence): _____
_____

    D. Supporting Evidence: _____
_____

Explanation (Explain how this supports the topic sentence): _____
_____

    E. Supporting Evidence: _____
_____

Explanation (Explain how this supports the topic sentence): _____
_____

II. Closer: Show how A and B support the topic sentence: _____
_____

Write the source:_____

Remaining Body Paragraphs.
Follow the same structure as paragraph II.

Paragraph V. Conclusion
I. Restate thesis statement: _____
_____
_____

II. Strong statement that shows how the topic sentences support the thesis: _____
_____
_____

Chapter V: Grading Rubrics

One-Paragraph Essay Grading Rubric

Grading Scale
4   Exceeds Standards
3   Meets Standards
2   Approaching Standards
1   Below Standards
0   Nonexistent

Y/N

I.   Thesis Statement:
Does it persuasively answer the question?   _____
               Score _____

II.   Evidence Used:
Are two or more relevant pieces of evidence used?   _____
               Score _____

III.   Evidence Explained
Is the evidence explained correctly and persuasively?   _____
               Score _____

IV.   Conclusion:
Does the evidence strengthen the topic sentence?   _____
               Score _____

V.   Prewriting Activities
Are all prewriting activities included and attached
to the final?   _____
               Score _____

Total Addition of Scores =   _____
               <u>X 5</u>
       Score =   _____
Spelling or Grammatical Errors   -_____
Missing Prewriting Work   -_____

Final Score =   _____

Five-Paragraph Essay Grading Rubric

Grading Scale
4   Exceeds Standards
3   Meets Standards
2   Approaching Standards
1   Below Standards
0   Nonexistent

Paragraph I.   Yes/No
A. Thesis: Does it answer the question and provide organizational structure?   _____
B. Interest?   Does it grab the interest of the reader?   _____
                               Score: _____

Paragraph II.
A. Topic Sentence: Does it provide a strong statement supporting the thesis?   _____
B. Evidence: 1. Is evidence used to support the topic sentence?   _____
                2. Is the evidence explained clearly and in detail?   _____
C. Closer: Does the closer convincingly link the paragraph's evidence
       with the topic sentence?   _____
                               Score: _____

Paragraph III.
A. Topic Sentence: Does it provide a strong statement supporting the thesis?   _____
B. Evidence: 1. Is evidence used to support the topic sentence?   _____
                2. Is the evidence explained clearly and in detail?   _____
C. Closer: Does the closer convincingly link the paragraph's evidence
       with the topic sentence?   _____
                               Score: _____

Paragraph IV.
A. Topic Sentence: Does it provide a strong statement supporting the thesis?   _____
B. Evidence: 1. Is evidence used to support the topic sentence?   _____
                2. Is the evidence explained clearly and in detail?   _____
C. Closer: Does the closer convincingly link the evidence
       with the topic sentence?   _____
                               Score: _____

Paragraph V.
A. Restating Topic Sentences: Are the topic sentences in II, III, IV restated?   _____
B.   Closer: Does the Closer persuasively show that the main ideas of
     paragraphs II, III, and IV strongly support the thesis?   _____

                          Score: _____ X 5 = _____
           Spelling or Grammatical Errors   -_____
           Missing Prewriting Work   -_____

           Total Score   _____

Social Studies - Multi-Page Research Essay Grading Rubric

Grading Scale

4 Exceeds Standards
3 Meets Standards
2 Approaching Standards
1 Below Standards
0 Nonexistent

I. Organization/Structure of the Essay Y/N

A. Thesis: Does the thesis take a firm position on the essay topic? _____

B. Topic Sentences: Do topic sentences strongly support the thesis? _____

C. Conclusion: Does the conclusion persuasively affirm the thesis? _____

Score: _____

II Evidence: Part I: Accuracy and Adequacy of Evidence

A. Accuracy: Is all evidence accurate (true)? _____

B. Adequacy: Is enough evidence used? _____

Score: _____

III Evidence: Part II: Validity and Persuasiveness of Evidence

B. Validity: Do explanations of evidence make sense? _____

A. Persuasiveness: Do explanations of evidence support main ideas? _____

Score: _____

IV Language Mechanics

A. Punctuation: Does the essay use correct punctuation? _____

B. Grammar: Does the essay use correct grammar (sentence structure)? _____

C. Spelling: Is spelling correct? _____

Score: _____

V Writing Process

A. Prewriting Activities: Are all prewriting activities complete? _____

B. Effort: Is great effort shown in these activities? _____

Score: _____

Total Score: _____ X 5 = Grade: _____